better together*

*This book is best read together, grownup and kid.

 akidsco.com

a
kids
book
about

a kids book about

alzheimer's

by Tanya Iovino & Kiki Kouris

A Kids Co.
Editor Emma Wolf
Designer Duke Stebbins
Creative Director Rick DeLucco
Studio Manager Kenya Feldes
Sales Director Melanie Wilkins
Head of Books Jennifer Goldstein
CEO and Founder Jelani Memory

DK
Delhi Technical Team Bimlesh Tiwary Pushpak Tyagi, Rakesh Kumar
Senior Production Editor Jennifer Murray
Senior Production Controller Louise Minihane
Senior Acquisitions Editor Katy Flint
Acquisitions Project Editor Sara Forster
Managing Art Editor Vicky Short
Managing Director, Licensing Mark Searle

First American edition, 2025
Published in the United States by DK Publishing, 1745 Broadway, 20th Floor,
New York, NY 10019

First published in Great Britain in 2025 by
Dorling Kindersley Limited, 20 Vauxhall Bridge Road, London SW1V 2SA
A Penguin Random House Company

The authorised representative in the EEA is
Dorling Kindersley Verlag GmbH. Arnulfstr. 124, 80636 Munich, Germany

A catalog record for this book is available from the Library of Congress.
A CIP catalogue record for this book is available from the British Library.
ISBN: 978-0-2417-4387-4

DK books are available at special discounts when purchased in bulk for sales
promotions, premiums, fund-raising, or education use. For details, contact:
DK Publishing Special Markets, 1745 Broadway, 20th Floor, New York, NY 10019
SpecialSales@dk.com

Printed and bound in China
www.dk.com
akidsco.com

For our mom, Elaine;
the best pappou in the world, Peter;
and Tanya's husband, Nick,
for their endless support
throughout the years.

They are our #1 cheerleaders in life, and
we would be nowhere without them.

We also send special gratitude to our
friends and family for always encouraging
and supporting our advocacy.

Intro
for grownups

If you're reading this book, it's probably because Alzheimer's disease personally impacts you or someone you know. Trust us—we know this can be a weighty topic, and the amount of uncertainty that comes with this disease feels endless.

The fact that you are here means you care about this disease and the people impacted by it, and we want you to know that you are not alone. Talking to your kids about Alzheimer's may seem tricky because there is no one-size-fits-all answer to their questions. We hope this book helps you navigate those unknowns and recognize that you are part of a support system spanning millions of people experiencing what you are living through today.

Hi.

My name is Kiki.

And my name is Tanya.

We're sisters
(and best friends!).

We're both funny and stubborn.

We're passionate people and **VERY LOUD!**

We both love to dance and cook.

We also love to travel—especially to Greece! Because that's where our family is from.

Part of our Greek culture is being super close with family.

This means growing up, we were with our aunts, uncles, cousins, and grandparents all the time.

IT WAS THE BEST!

We were especially close with our grandma (yiayia, or Γιαγιά, in Greek) and grandpa (pappou, or Παππού).

They met and got married in Greece
(which is a really cute story for another time),
and then immigrated to Chicago to start
a new life and pursue their dreams.

Our yiayia was the matriarch* of our family.

She was loving, she had great skin,
and she was VERY stylish.

We actually still wear some of her
clothes and accessories!

*This means she was the head of our family.

She was so smart.

Yiayia didn't speak any English when she first came to America, but she watched TV and read books and magazines to teach herself.

Yiayia always had snacks for us, even if we hadn't eaten that long ago—Greek grandparents always make sure you're fed!

She would cook and bake for days before big holidays, and her food was absolutely delicious.

We loved her so much, and we felt lucky to live so close to her and Pappou.

They were like a second set of parents to us, and they loved each other *A LOT*.

But one day, Yiayia had a hard time remembering who Pappou was.

And that's when we knew something was wrong.

It happened so fast.

It felt like we went to bed one night,

woke up,

and our whole world had changed.

We didn't know it at the time,
but Yiayia had **Alzheimer's.**

Alzheimer's

is a disease that causes problems
with memory, thinking, and behavior.
It can impact every aspect of daily life.

Maybe you've heard of Alzheimer's
or the term "dementia" before.
Or maybe this is all new to you!

Dementia is a general term for loss of memory, language, and other thinking abilities.

Alzheimer's is the most common form of dementia.

Alzheimer's is a specific disease while dementia is not.

Alzheimer's cannot be prevented,
or cured, or slowed down (yet).

Alzheimer's is also not only an
older person's disease
(though a lot of people think it is!).

Alzheimer's is really hard to diagnose because everybody's experience is so different.

No two people have Alzheimer's
the exact same way.

Our sharp, loving, caring yiayia
quickly started to change.

She became emotional:
sad, upset, and scared.

She grew aggressive over time.

She would misplace and hide things.

She often didn't know where she was
(especially at night).

She forgot how to bake, cook,
dress herself, and speak English.

And the hardest thing for all of us
was that she forgot Pappou.

It's like she became a totally different
person and her whole personality changed.

When someone develops Alzheimer's, it can also mean:

Getting lost in a familiar neighborhood.

Not remembering how to drive a car.

No longer wanting to do work or spend time with loved ones.

Facing challenges in planning or solving problems.

Having difficulty with speaking, reading, and writing.

Forgetting names and important dates.

Misplacing things and not being able to think back to find them.

Everyday things (like teeth brushing) become really hard.

Feeling confused about time and place, like not knowing what day it is.

Experiencing sensory overload, which is when all 5 of someone's senses are activating at the same time in a way that feels overwhelming.

Listen, Alzheimer's is hard.

The thing about Alzheimer's
is that it affects everybody:
the person who has it and
all the people who love them.

Taking care of Yiayia was sad,
lonely, scary, and frustrating.

While it was one of the hardest parts of our lives, making sure that Yiayia felt comfortable and loved was one of the most important things we've ever done.

Because she always did that for us.

OK, that was a lot.

You probably have questions
(we had TONS of them).

Questions like:

When someone has Alzheimer's, are they a different person?

Do they still love me?

Am I still important to them?

What can I do to help?

We don't have all the answers.

Everything about Alzheimer's
is complicated and hard and
it's difficult to understand.

But we learned a lot
taking care of Yiayia that
we'd like to share with you.

First,

Alzheimer's disease is what the person has—it's not the person themselves.

The person you know is still there, but how they feel and act toward you and others is changed by the disease they have.

Second,

they will say things and do things that aren't like they used to, and sometimes that can make you feel scared or confused.

THEY are scared and confused too, and they absolutely do not mean to hurt you or make you sad.

Third,

it's important to remember that while they look the same on the outside their brain is changing on the inside.

But just because they don't remember you or your name doesn't mean they don't love you.

Our relationship with Yiayia changed
when she developed Alzheimer's.

She took care of us our whole lives,
and then we were taking care of her.

Each person's experience with Alzheimer's, and how their family handles it, is unique.

There isn't one *right way* to best care for somebody with Alzheimer's or a related dementia.

Try the best you can.

If you feel scared, or angry,
or lonely, that's totally normal.

Some days will be harder than others,
and your best is the best you can do.

Go along with how your person
sees and experiences the world.

We spent a lot of time trying
to help Yiayia remember.

But what was more helpful was to
just listen and be present with her.

Above all, keep them safe, comfortable, and most importantly, *love them*.

Know that you aren't alone in caring for your person with Alzheimer's.

Ask for help and extra support from the people you love, and check out all the great Alzheimer's resources available online.*

*We put some in the back of this book for you too.

Alzheimer's is so tough.

And it can get really easy to forget the great memories you've had with a person who has it.

But we think of Yiayia's warmth, passion, strength, and bravery, and we share her story so we never forget who she was before getting Alzheimer's.

Outro
for grownups

Now that you've read our story and learned about our family's experience with Alzheimer's disease, we hope that it reassures you that you are not alone in what you are experiencing, and we hope you find solace in what we've shared. We wrote this book to aid in breaking down the stigma that surrounds Alzheimer's and related dementias.

Alzheimer's is not a normal part of aging, and it is not just an older person's disease.

It is completely normal to feel scared, angry, sad, and every emotion in between—we know we did.

We learned that the best thing you can do is try your best to ensure that your loved one is safe and cared for and never forget how much they love you. They may have a hard time remembering your name, or they may act in ways that are completely outside their usual behavior, but the love they have for you will never be taken away by this disease.

Alzheimer's Association: www.alz.org

Women's Alzheimer's Movement:
thewomensalzheimersmovement.org

HFC: wearehfc.org

National Institute on Aging:
www.nia.nih.gov/health/alzheimers

Made to empower.

a kids book about **racism**
by Jelani Memory

a kids book about ANXIETY
by Ross Szabo

a kids book about DISABILITY
by Kristine Napper

a kids book about IMAGINATION
by LEVAR BURTON

a kids book about belonging
by Kevin Carroll

a kids book about failure
by Dr. Laymon Hicks

a kids book about GRATITUDE
by Ben Kenyon

a kids book about LIFE ONLINE
by Dave S. Anderson & Blake Fleischacker

a kids book about body image
by Rebecca Alexander

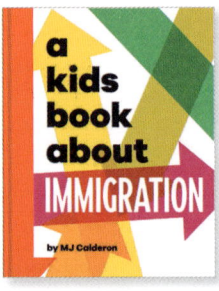
a kids book about IMMIGRATION
by MJ Calderon

a kids book about EMPATHY
by Daron K. Roberts

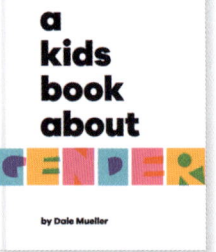
a kids book about GENDER
by Dale Mueller

a kids book about Love
by ZIGGY MARLEY

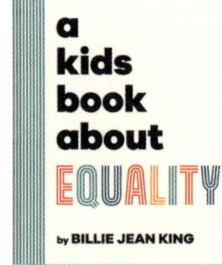
a kids book about EQUALITY
by BILLIE JEAN KING

a kids book about MONEY
by Adam Stramwasser

a kids book about FEMINISM
by Emma McIlroy

a kids book about adventure
by Dr. Ben Tertin

a kids book about CLIMATE CHANGE
by Zanagee Artis Olivia Greenspan

a kids book about CONFIDENCE
by Joy Cho

a kids book about BEING NONBINARY
by Hunter Chinn-Raicht

Discover more at akidsco.com